MELODIC MOTION STUDIES FOR DRUMSET

Directional Strategies for Exploring New Sounds from Familiar Stickings

BY JEFF SALISBURY

EDITED BY RICK MATTINGLY

To access audio visit:
www.halleonard.com/mylibrary

5986-1604-8974-9687

The audio tracks were recorded by Joe Capps
at Poker Hill Studio, Underhill, Vermont

ISBN 978-1-4803-5467-8

CORPORATION
7777 W. BLUEMOUND RD. P.O. BOX 13819 MILWAUKEE, WI 53213

In Australia Contact:
Hal Leonard Australia Pty. Ltd.
4 Lentara Court
Cheltenham, Victoria, 3192 Australia
Email: ausadmin@halleonard.com.au

Visit Hal Leonard Online at
www.halleonard.com

ACKNOWLEDGEMENTS

Thanks to all my family, teachers, students past and present, and colleagues over the years. Linda McDavitt, Bert Brewer, John Pearson, and Albert King deserve special thanks for their essential roles in my early musical growth. John S. Pratt has been an enduring source of inspiration. His gracious hospitality and flow of information will never be forgotten. I owe so much to the life's work of Alan Dawson and George Lawrence Stone, whose musical legacy will span the globe forever. Thanks to Ben Hans and Jeff Schroedl for giving me a chance. I also wish to thank the KoSA family, who have enriched my life immensely.

PREFACE

This book examines some of the infinite possibilities relating sound to motion that I have worked on over the past fifteen years. It is the culmination of numerous studies using circular, vertical, horizontal, diagonal, and various combinations of these motions to develop freedom of movement on the drums. I hope that by working through these exercises, new perspectives can be opened, and that we can discover new ways to utilize familiar techniques.

ABOUT THE AUTHOR

Jeff Salisbury teaches drumset at the University of Vermont and is an original faculty member of KoSA Percussion Workshops. He studied with George Marsh, Peter Magadini, Bob Moses, and Max Roach. He has played professionally since the 1960s, and has performed, toured, and recorded with numerous blues, rhythm & blues, and jazz artists over the years, including Albert King, Cold Blood, Linda Tillery, Chuck Berry, Bo Diddley, and others. He maintains an active teaching and performing schedule, and he endorses DW drums and hardware.

Photo courtesy of Peter Wilder

CONTENTS

Notation Key

This book uses the Percussive Arts Society's *Standardized Drumset Notation* developed by Norman Weinberg.

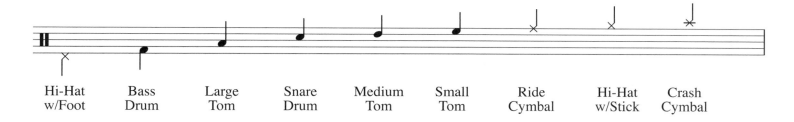

Hi-Hat w/Foot   Bass Drum   Large Tom   Snare Drum   Medium Tom   Small Tom   Ride Cymbal   Hi-Hat w/Stick   Crash Cymbal

PART ONE: STICKING AROUND THE CLOCK

Clockwise and Counterclockwise Movement Combinations

All of these exercises are based on the four possible combinations of clockwise and counterclockwise motion around the drums. As written, none of these incorporate cymbals or other sounds, but feel free to extrapolate to create whatever tonal colors please you.

The stickings used in this section all form even, one-measure phrases. Longer phrases will be examined later.

Exercise 1

Right hand counterclockwise; left hand clockwise; opposite for left-handed sets. Single strokes around the drums using four starting points for the lead hand.

Some rather cumbersome crosses occur that need to be dealt with. The first is between small and medium toms in the first rotation. I prefer to cross my right hand over my left in this case. In fact, my right hand crosses over my left in all of exercises 1 and 2.

In order to link the four parts of this exercise, move diagonally across the drumset from the last drum played by the lead hand—snare to medium tom, etc. Soft mallets lend a pleasant texture to all of these exercises.

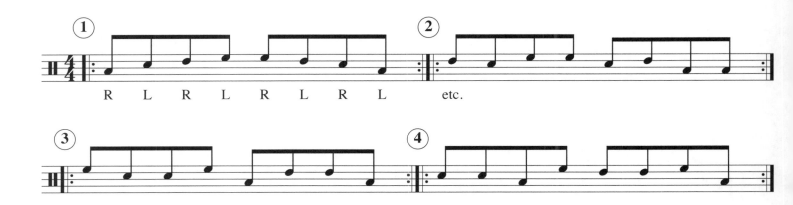

Exercise 2

Right hand clockwise; left hand counterclockwise. To connect the four parts, keep the lead hand on the drum played last.

Exercise 3

Both hands counterclockwise. I cross my left hand over my right for these, but see which you prefer. To connect, move diagonally as in example 1.

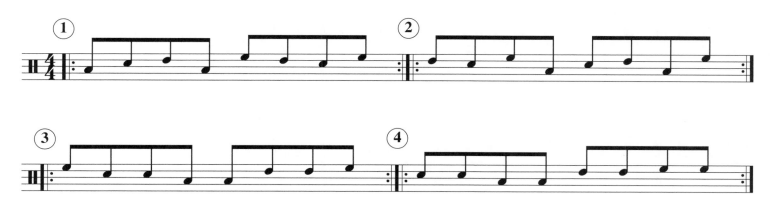

Exercise 4

Both hands clockwise. Connect as in example 2.

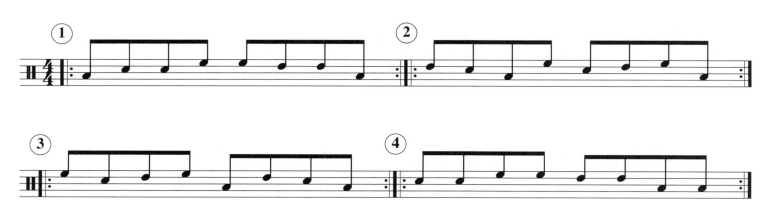

Exercise 5

Paradiddle-diddles using the four combinations of clockwise and counterclockwise motion.

R L R R L L R L R R L L etc.

Exercise 6

Paradiddle-diddles plus two sixteenth notes on the bass drum.

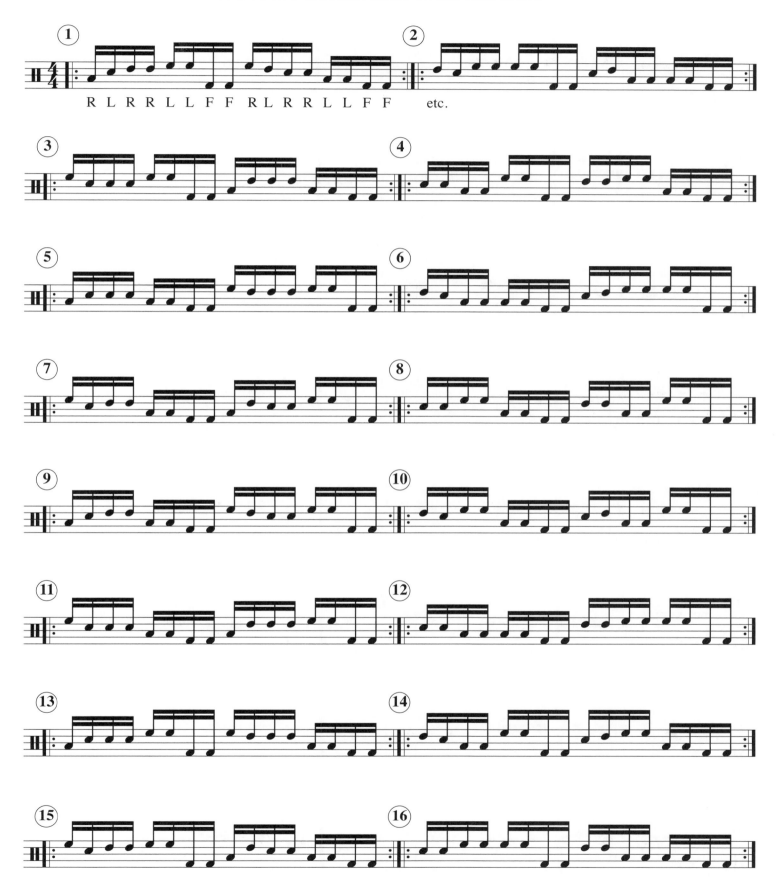

Exercise 7

Quintuplets using a single stroke and double stroke in the hands with a double on the bass drum.

R L L F F   R L L F F   R L L F F   R L L F F   etc.

Exercise 8

Four singles and four doubles as triplets in the hands.

R L R L R R L L R R L L   etc.

Exercise 9

Inverted double strokes in a sixteenth-note pulse.

R L L R R L L R R L L R R L L R   etc.

Exercise 10

One single and three doubles in the hands, plus a double on the bass drum. This rotation takes six beats of eighth-note triplets to complete.

Exercise 11

Four singles in the hands plus a double on the bass.

Exercise 12

Seven singles plus one double in a nine-note sequence.

PART TWO: VERTICAL, HORIZONTAL, AND DIAGONAL INVERSIONS OF PARADIDDLE-DIDDLES

Explorations of the paradiddle-diddle using the twelve possible inversions of the figure.

Exercise 13

Single strokes on medium and small toms; double strokes on floor tom and snare.

Forward and backward motion is employed here.

Exercise 14

Single strokes on floor tom and snare; doubles on medium and small toms.

Exercise 15

Single strokes on floor tom and medium tom; doubles on snare and small tom.

Lateral motion is explored here.

Exercise 16

Single strokes on snare and small tom; doubles on floor and medium toms.

Exercise 17

X-shaped motions are examined in exercises 17 and 18. In 17, the lead hand plays medium tom and snare, while the other hand plays small tom and floor tom. A counterclockwise motion works when the right hand starts the single strokes, and clockwise motion works when the left hand starts them. Singles are on the medium and small toms, doubles on the snare and floor tom.

Exercise 18

Single strokes on snare and floor tom; doubles on medium and small toms.

PART THREE: OUTSOURCING OF THE PARADIDDLE

Voicing paradiddle inversions on multiple sound sources.

Single paradiddle and inversions:

R L R R   L R L L

R L L R   L R R L

R R L R   L L R L

R L R L   L R L R

Exercise 19

Lead hand plays between ride cymbal and floor tom; the other hand plays between hi-hat and snare.

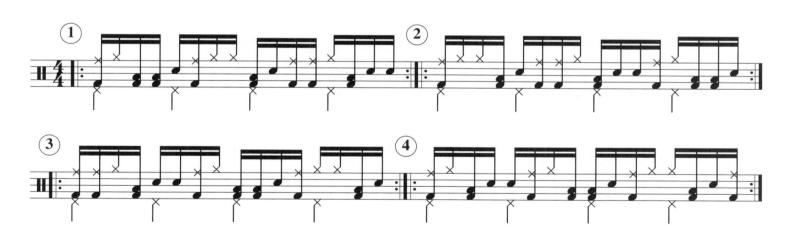

Exercise 20

Lead hand cycles among ride cymbal, medium tom, and floor tom; the other hand plays between hi-hat and snare.

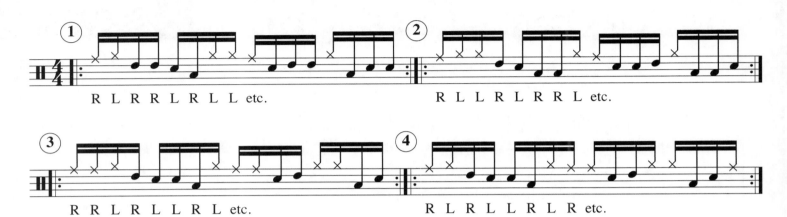

① R L R R L R L L etc. ② R L L R L R R L etc.

③ R R L R L L R L etc. ④ R L R L L R L R etc.

Exercise 21

Lead hand plays between ride cymbal and floor tom; the other hand cycles among hi-hat, snare, and small tom.

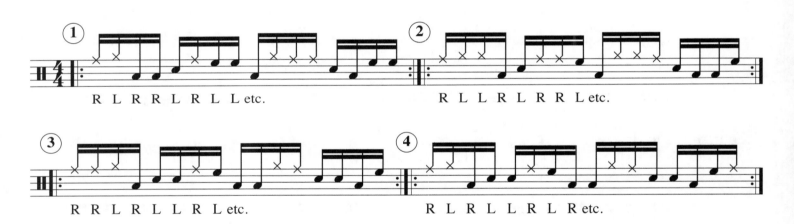

① R L R R L R L L etc. ② R L L R L R R L etc.

③ R R L R L L R L etc. ④ R L R L L R L R etc.

Exercise 22

Lead hand cycles through ride cymbal and medium, small, and floor toms; the other hand alternates between hi-hat and snare.

R L R R L R L L etc.

R L L R L R R L etc.

R R L R L L R L etc.

R L R L L R L R etc.

Exercise 23

Each hand plays three sound sources. Lead hand: ride, medium tom, floor tom. Other hand: hi-hat, snare, small tom.

R L R R L R L L etc.   R L L R L R R L etc.

R R L R L L R L etc.   R L R L L R L R etc.

Exercise 24

Lead hand plays four sources; the other hand plays three. The starting point of the lead hand changes for each inversion.

R R L R L L R L etc.

R L R L L R L R etc.

Exercise 25

Both hands play four sound sources; lead hand changes starting positions.

R L R R L R L L etc.

R L L R L R R L etc.

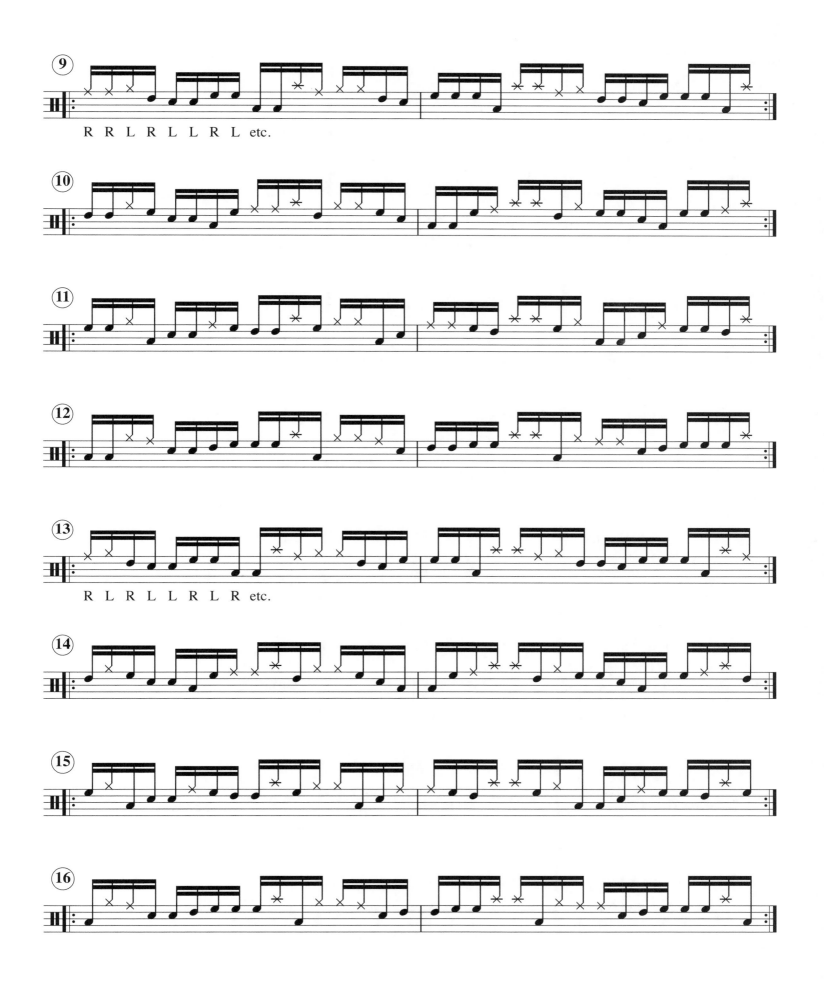

R R L R L L R L etc.

R L R L L L R L R etc.

Exercise 26

Still four sources for each hand, but the other hand changes starting positions.

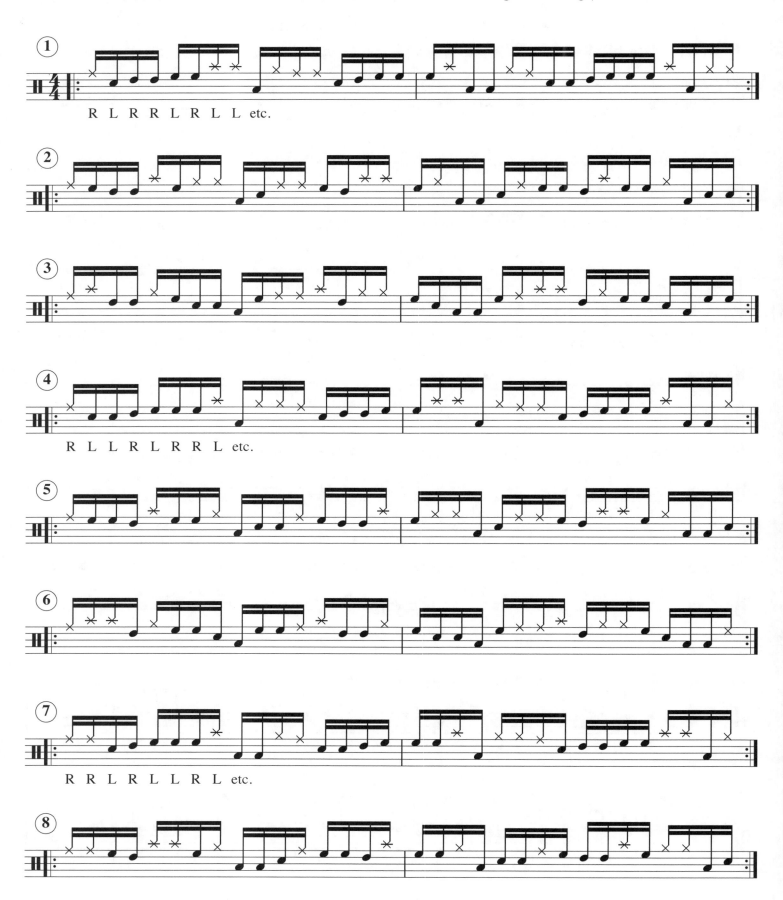

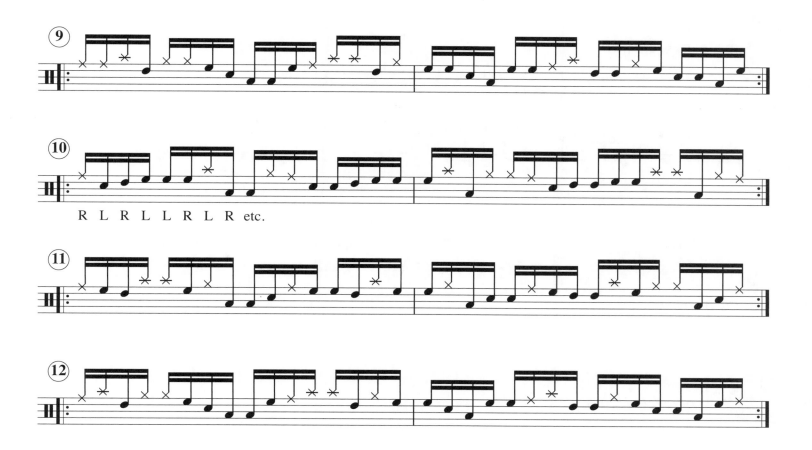

⑨

⑩

R L R L L R L R etc.

⑪

⑫

Exercise 27

"Parallel-a-diddles." This uses parallel, lateral motion to explore the single paradiddle inversions. The lead hand plays across the upper level of the set, from ride to medium and small toms to crash cymbal and back. The other hand plays from hi-hat to snare to floor tom and back. To compensate for fewer voices on the lower level, play two groups of notes on the floor tom; then, upon returning, play two groups on the hi-hat.

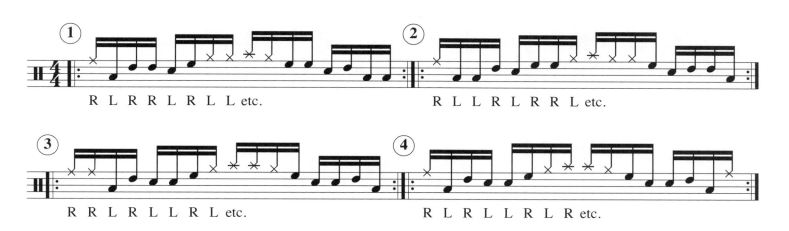

①

R L R R L R L L etc.

②

R L L R L R R L etc.

③

R R L R L L R L etc.

④

R L R L L R L R etc.

Exercise 28

Start from opposite sides of the drumset to play this variation.

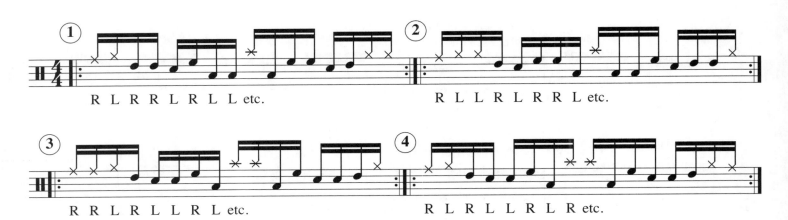

① R L R R L R L L etc.

② R L L R L R R L etc.

③ R R L R L L R L etc.

④ R L R L L R L R etc.

Exercise 29

Double paradiddles and inversions moving from opposite sides of the set.

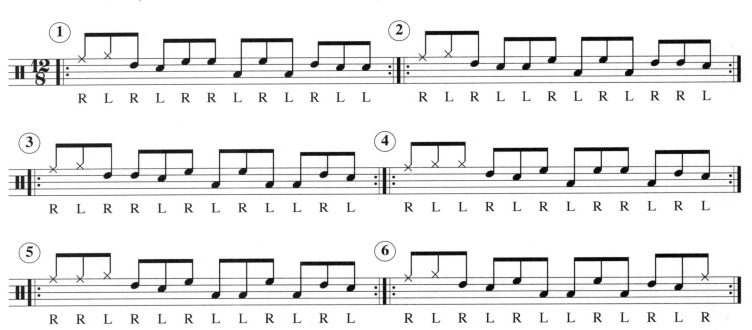

① R L R L R R L R L R L L

② R L R L L R L R L R R L

③ R L R R L R L R L L R L

④ R L L R L R L R R L R L

⑤ R R L R L R L L R L R L

⑥ R L R L R L L R L R L R

Exercise 30

Triple paradiddles and inversions move from opposite sides of the drumset.

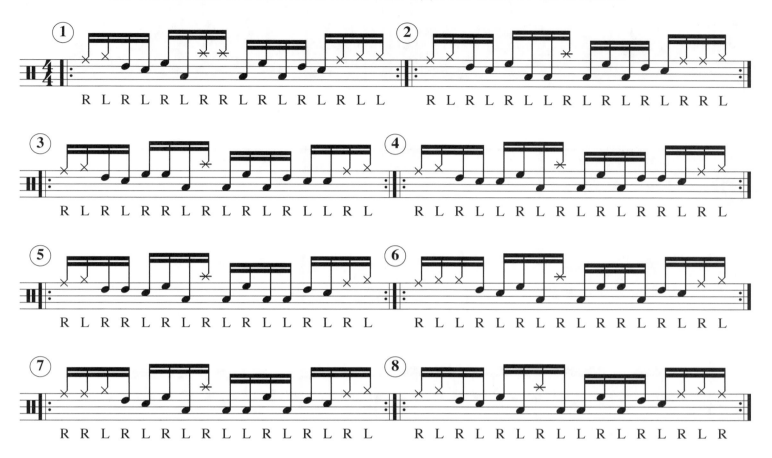

① R L R L R L R R L R L R L R L L

② R L R L R L L R L R L R L R R L

③ R L R L R R L R L R L R L L R L

④ R L R L L R L R L R L R R L R L

⑤ R L R R L R L R L R L L R L R L

⑥ R L L R L R L R L R R L R L R L

⑦ R R L R L R L R L L R L R L R L

⑧ R L R L R L R L L R L R L R L R

Exercise 31

Paradiddle-diddles across the set.

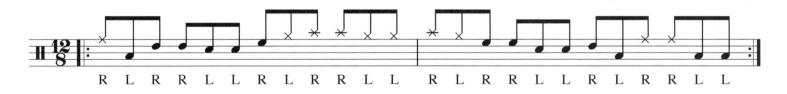

R L R R L L R L R L R R L L   R L R R L L R L R L R R L L

PART FOUR: BLOWING IN THE WINDMILLS

Exploring some possibilities of motion using single and double flammed mills

Exercise 32

The first measure of each inversion has the lead hand moving among the medium tom, small tom, and snare while the other hand accompanies on the hi-hat. The second measure has the other hand moving among two toms and snare while the lead hand accompanies on the ride cymbal. The third measure combines two beats each of the previous movements. For the rest of the book, the letter "B" (for "both") is used to designate flams.

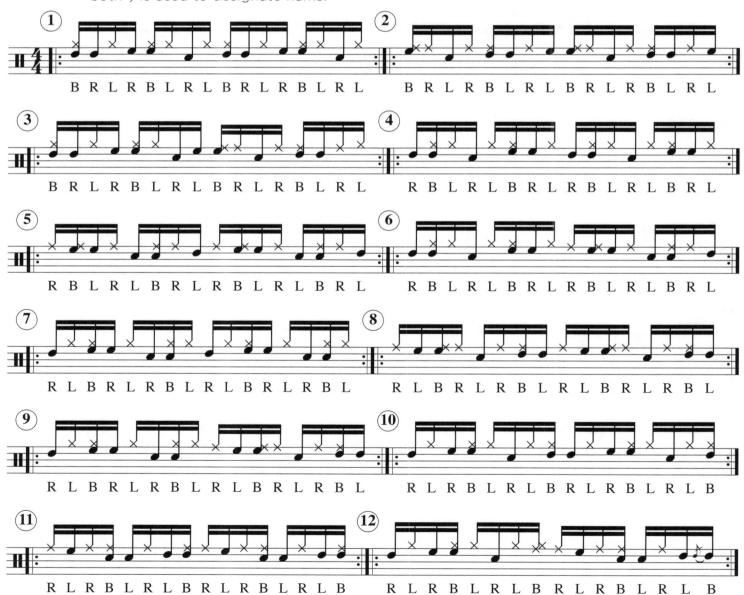

1. B R L R B L R L B R L R B L R L

2. B R L R B L R L B R L R B L R L

3. B R L R B L R L B R L R B L R L

4. R B L R L B R L R B L R L B R L

5. R B L R L B R L R B L R L B R L

6. R B L R L B R L R B L R L B R L

7. R L B R L R B L R L B R L R B L

8. R L B R L R B L R L B R L R B L

9. R L B R L R B L R L B R L R B L

10. R L R B L R L B R L R B L R L B

11. R L R B L R L B R L R B L R L B

12. R L R B L R L B R L R B L R L B

Exercise 33

Now the single flammed mill is played in a triplet pulse with the lead hand moving from floor to medium to small toms, finishing with the floor tom. The other hand plays the hi-hat, then switches to the toms for the second measure, accompanied by the lead hand on the ride cymbal.

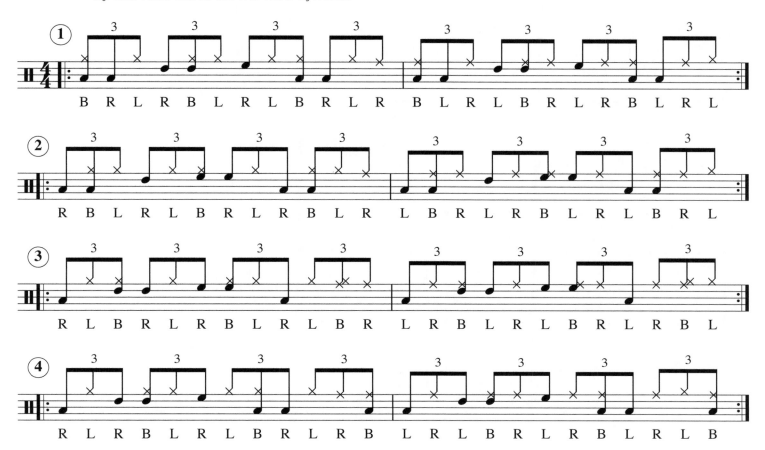

Try this "4 over 3" bass drum/hi-hat pattern with the above patterns.

Exercise 34

The lead hand starts on the ride cymbal while the other hand plays the melody in the first measure; then the lead hand plays the melody while the other hand plays the hi-hat in the second measure.

Double flammed mills are played in two-measure triplet melodies, with each exercise representing an inversion of the sticking.

Exercise 35

Exercise 35/40
0:00–0:52

Exercise 36

R B L R L R L B R L R L   etc.

Exercise 37

R L B R L R L R B L R L   etc.

Exercise 38

Exercise 39

R L R L B R L R L R B L   etc.

Exercise 40

Exercise 35/40
0:54–1:38

(1) R L R L R B L R L R L B   etc.

Optional Foot Patterns for Paradiddle Triplet Melodies

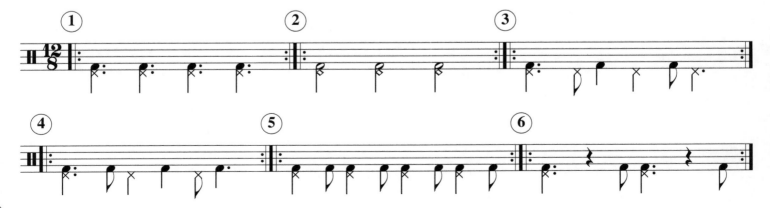

PART FIVE: LEAVE NO "STONE" UNTURNED

Miscellaneous Motion Variations of Familiar Patterns

This section consists of a variety of exercises that do not fit easily under previous headings.

Exercise 41

This is based on exercise 33 from George Lawrence Stone's *Stick Control* with four voices for each hand.

Exercise 42

Now we use a pattern based on exercise 43 from *Stick Control* in the same manner.

R L L R L L R L R L L R L L R L etc.

Exercise 43

Double paradiddles using five voices for each hand.

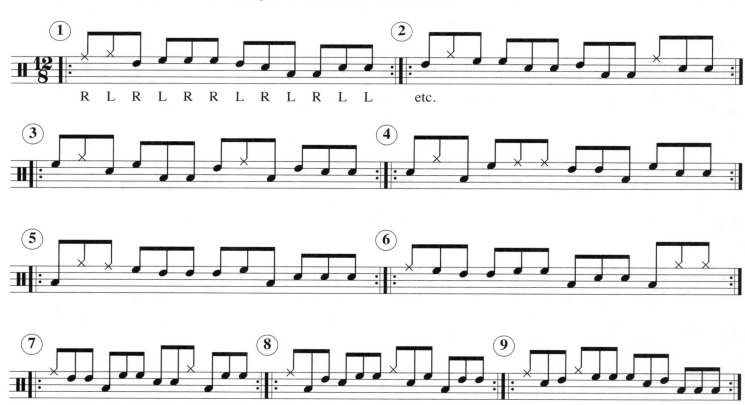

R L R L R R L R L R L L etc.

Exercise 44

Double paradiddles with five voices for the lead hand and two voices for the other hand.

R L R L R R L R L R L L   etc.

Exercise 45

Five voices for the lead hand and an L-shaped, three-voice figure for the other hand.

Exercise 46

This exercise moves some familiar sticking patterns using two voices each (RLLR LLRL, RLRR LRRL, paradiddle inversions, and single flammed mills) in an up-and-down motion.

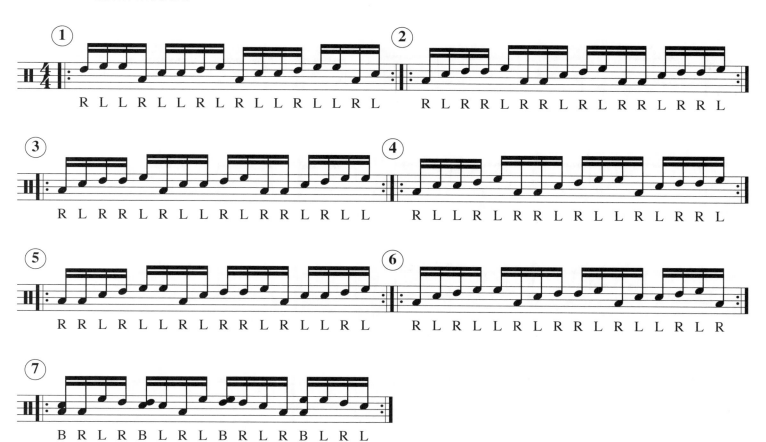

① R L L R L L R L R L L R L L R L

② R L R R L R R L R L R R L R R L

③ R L R R L R L L R L R R L R L L

④ R L L R L R R L R L L L R L R R L

⑤ R R L R L L R L R R L R L L R L

⑥ R L R L L R L R R L R L L R L R

⑦ B R L R B L R L B R L R B L R L

Exercise 47

Single paradiddles as triplets form melodies around the toms with one hand while the other hand plays accompaniment on cymbals. The melodies switch from hand to hand every three paradiddles.

Exercise 48

A jazz ride ostinato is played over half-note, quarter-note, eighth-note, and sixteenth-note triplets as single strokes, then double strokes between the snare and bass drum.

PART SIX: TILTING AT WINDMILLS OR PLAYING THE NUMBERS

This section examines the six double flammed mill inversions, then takes them apart and puts them together again. We then combine two double flammed mills and one single flammed mill in three different orders. If we use the number 6 to represent the double flammed mill and the number 4 to represent the single flammed mill, we can put them together as 6/6/4, 6/4/6, and 4/6/6. Each of these sequences is then inverted six ways and revoiced on the drumset, yielding some intriguing possibilities.

Exercise 49

Here are the six sticking permutations for the double flammed mill, which can reveal many rhythmic possibilities when revoiced on two or more sound sources. It helps to become accustomed to playing through the inversions on one sound source prior to separating the hands.

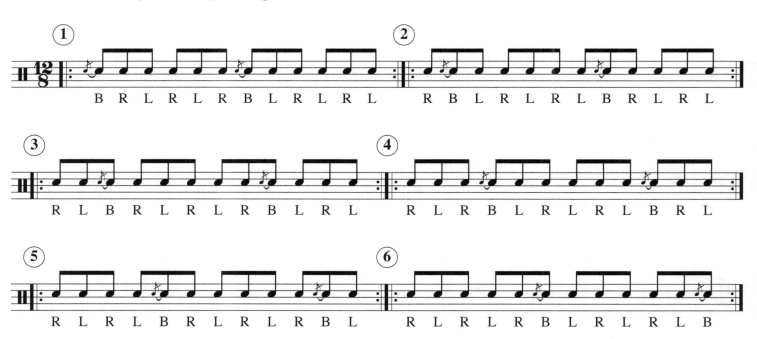

Exercise 50

After achieving a comfort level with exercise 49, try playing the rudiment on two
voices—hi-hat and snare, ride and snare, or any other components you prefer.

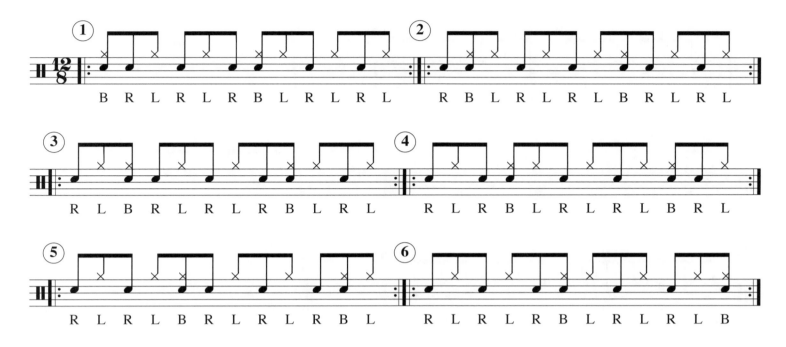

① B R L R L R B L R L R L ② R B L R L R L B R L R L

③ R L B R L R L R B L R L ④ R L R B L R L R L B R L

⑤ R L R L B R L R L R B L ⑥ R L R L R B L R L R L B

Exercise 51

Here again are the six inversions, now dissected to show possible revoicings for each hand, then the combination of the two-hand parts.

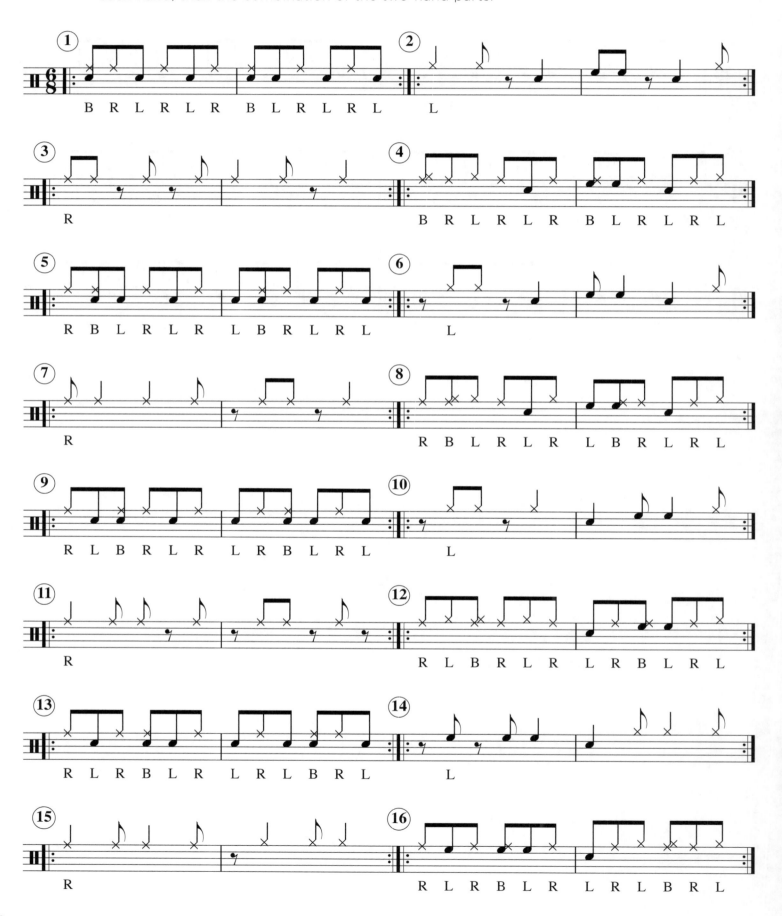

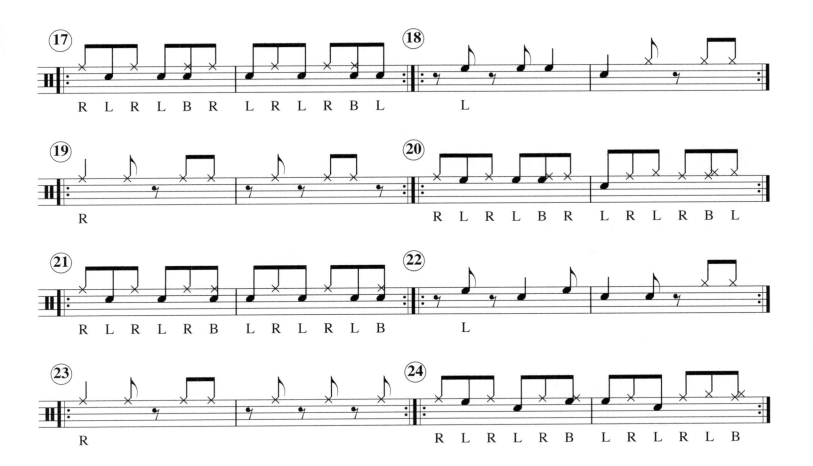

Exercise 52

Now we combine two double flammed mills and one single flammed mill in all inversions of 6/6/4, 6/4/6, and 4/6/6 on the snare. All stickings reverse on the repeats.

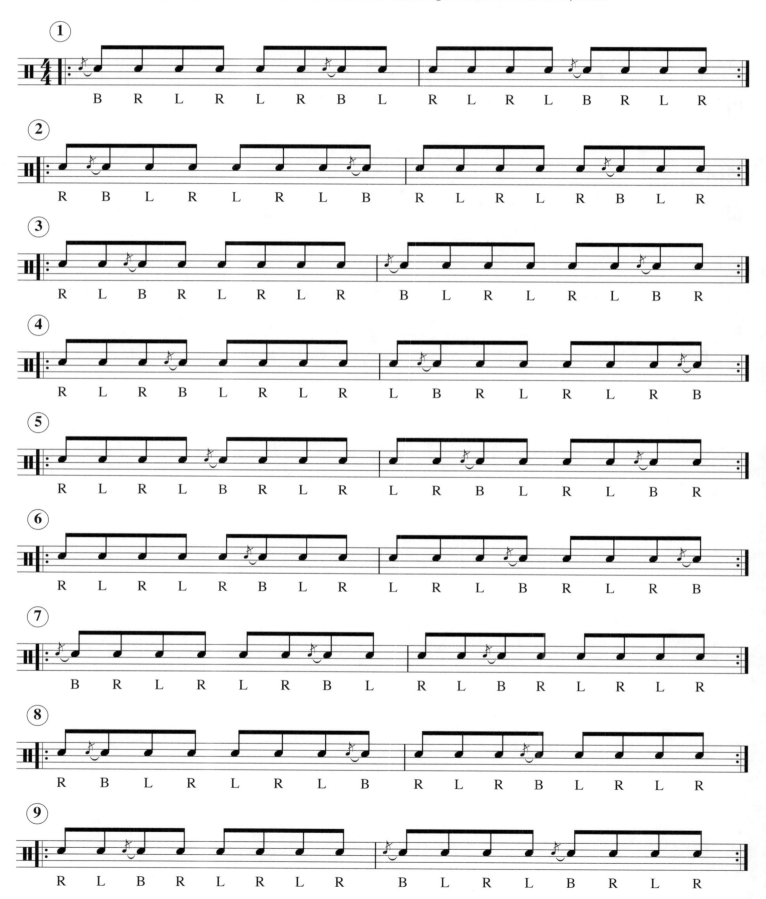

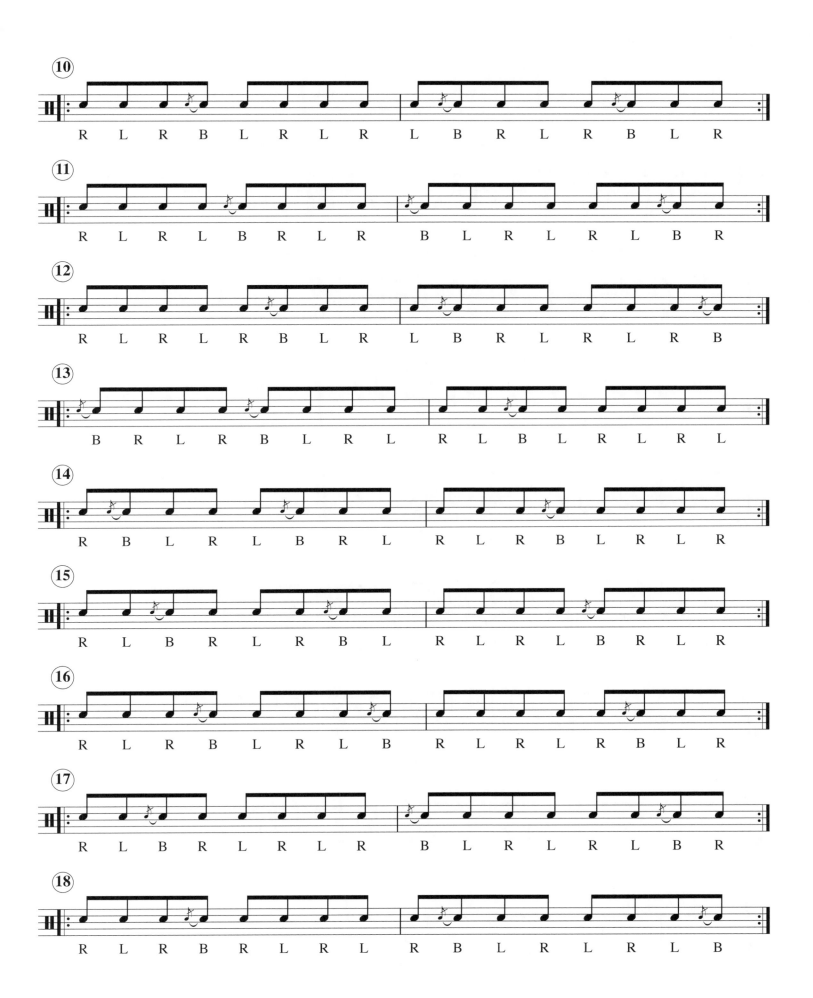

Exercise 53 "Windmill"

These stickings are in 6/6/4 order, with each inversion followed by revoicing on the drumset.

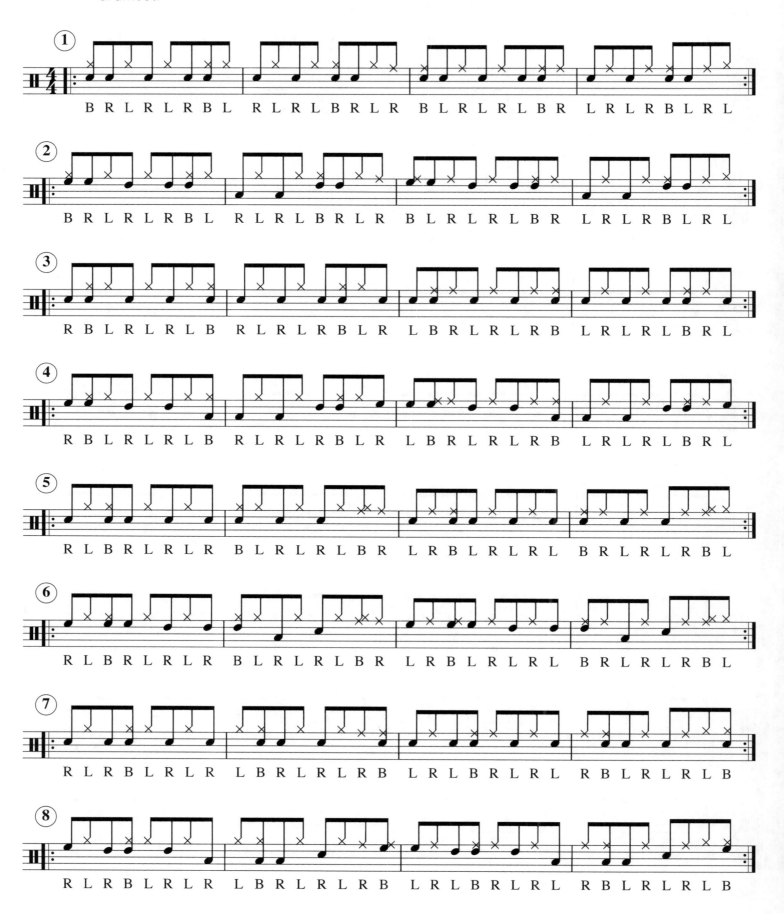

① B R L R L R B L   R L R L B R L R   B L R L R L B R   L R L R B L R L

② B R L R L R B L   R L R L B R L R   B L R L R L B R   L R L R B L R L

③ R B L R L R L B   R L R L R B L R   L B R L R L R B   L R L R L B R L

④ R B L R L R L B   R L R L R B L R   L B R L R L R B   L R L R L B R L

⑤ R L B R L R L R   B L R L R L B R   L R B L R L R L   B R L R L R B L

⑥ R L B R L R L R   B L R L R L B R   L R B L R L R L   B R L R L R B L

⑦ R L R B L R L R   L B R L R L R B   L R L B R L R L   R B L R L R L B

⑧ R L R B L R L R   L B R L R L R B   L R L B R L R L   R B L R L R L B

9

R L R L B R L R   L R B L R L B R   L R L R B L R L   R L B R L R B L

10

R L R L B R L R   L R B L R L B R   L R L R B L R L   R L B R L R B L

11

R L R L R B L R   L R L B R L R B   L R L R L B R L   R L R B L R L B

12

R L R L R B L R   L R L B R L R B   L R L R L B R L   R L R B L R L B

Exercise 54

This is the same 6/6/4 order as the previous exercise, with the opposite hand beginning the melody.

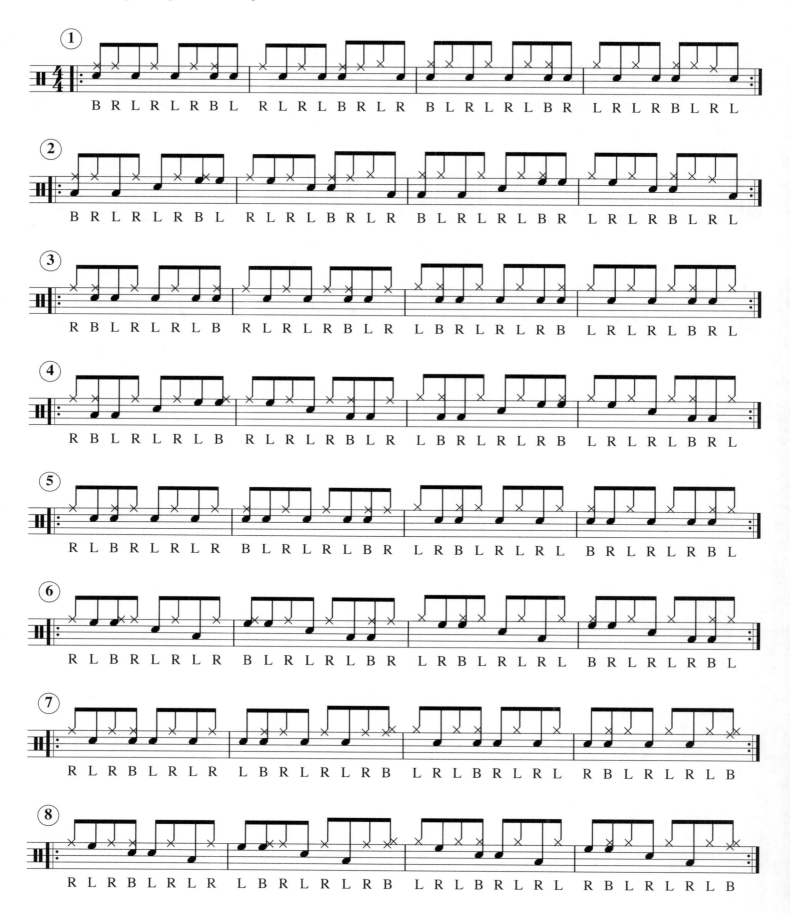

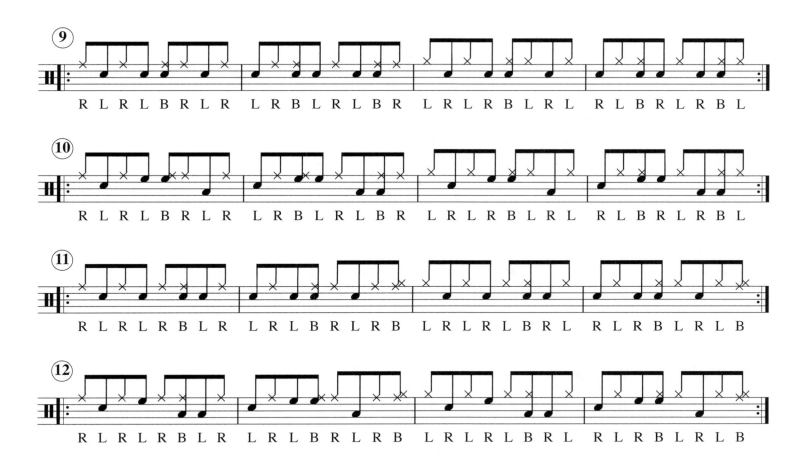

9

R L R L B R L R   L R B L R L B R   L R L R B L R L   R L B R L R B L

10

R L R L B R L R   L R B L R L B R   L R L R B L R L   R L B R L R B L

11

R L R L R B L R   L R L B R L R B   L R L R L B R L   R L R B L R L B

12

R L R L R B L R   L R L B R L R B   L R L R L B R L   R L R B L R L B

Exercise 55

6/4/6 order, following the same procedure as exercise 53.

Exercise 56

6/4/6 order with the opposite hand beginning the melody.

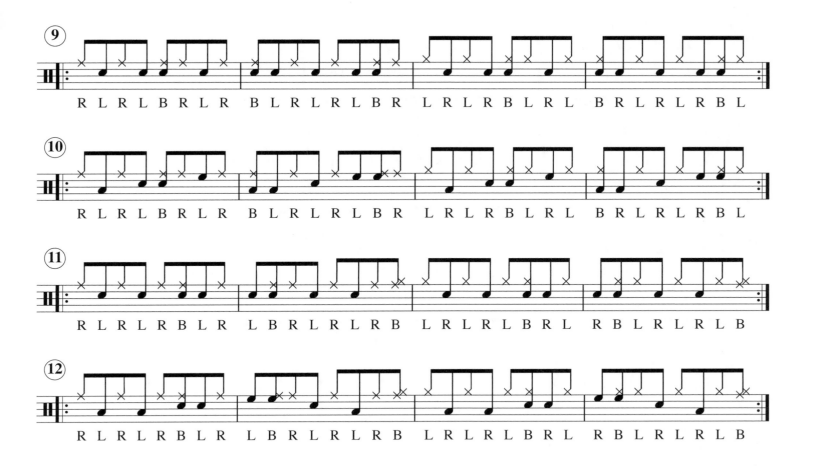

Exercise 57

4/6/6 order, using the same strategy as examples 53 and 55.

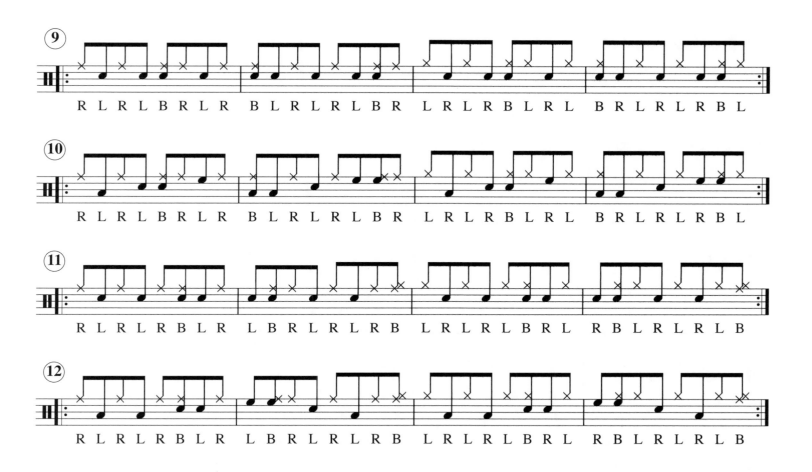

⑨ R L R L B R L R   B L R L R L B R   L R L R B L R L   B R L R L R B L

⑩ R L R L B R L R   B L R L R L B R   L R L R B L R L   B R L R L R B L

⑪ R L R L R B L R   L B R L R L R B   L R L R L B R L   R B L R L R L B

⑫ R L R L R B L R   L B R L R L R B   L R L R L B R L   R B L R L R L B

Exercise 58

4/6/6 order with the opposite hand beginning the melody.

①

B R L R B L R L   R L B R L R L R   B L R L B R L R   L R B L R L R L

②

B R L R B L R L   R L B R L R L R   B L R L B R L R   L R B L R L R L

③

R B L R L B R L   R L R B L R L R   L B R L R B L R   L R L B R L R L

④

R B L R L B R L   R L R B L R L R   L B R L R B L R   L R L B R L R L

⑤

R L B R L R B L   R L R L B R L R   L R B L R L B R   L R L R B L R L

⑥

R L B R L R B L   R L R L B R L R   L R B L R L B R   L R L R B L R L

⑦

R L R B L R L B   R L R L R B L R   L R L B R L R B   L R L R L B R L

⑧

R L R B L R L B   R L R L R B L R   L R L B R L R B   L R L R L B R L

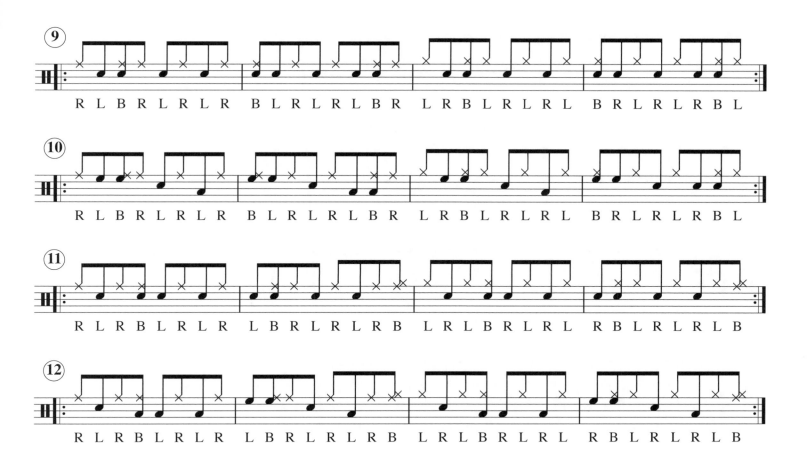

9

R L B R L R L R   B L R L R L B R   L R B L R L R L   B R L R L R B L

10

R L B R L R L R   B L R L R L B R   L R B L R L R L   B R L R L R B L

11

R L R B L R L R   L B R L R L R B   L R L B R L R L   R B L R L R L B

12

R L R B L R L R   L B R L R L R B   L R L B R L R L   R B L R L R L B

Exercise 59 Bossa/clave options

Here are three examples of Latin rhythms derived from these rudimental combinations.

The first has a bossa nova rhythm that can be played by splitting double strokes between the snare and toms. The second has 3–2 rumba clave by splitting the doubles between toms and snare. The third gives us a 3–2 cascara rhythm, switching after two measures to the opposite hand.

Exercise 60

Now we can substitute two Swiss Army triplets for one of the double flammed mills, giving some new possibilities. The sticking can be reversed to put the figures on the opposite hand.

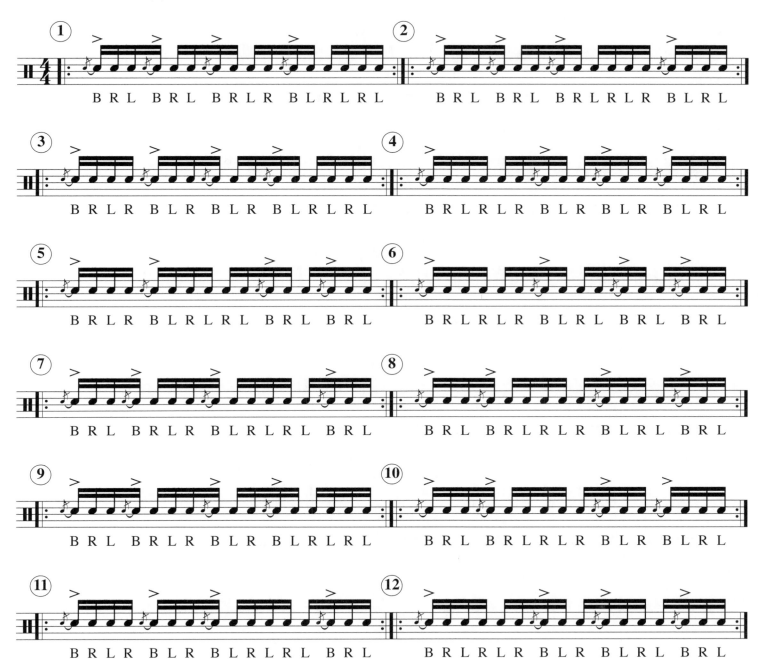

Exercise 61

These demonstrate the same stickings placed on two sound sources.

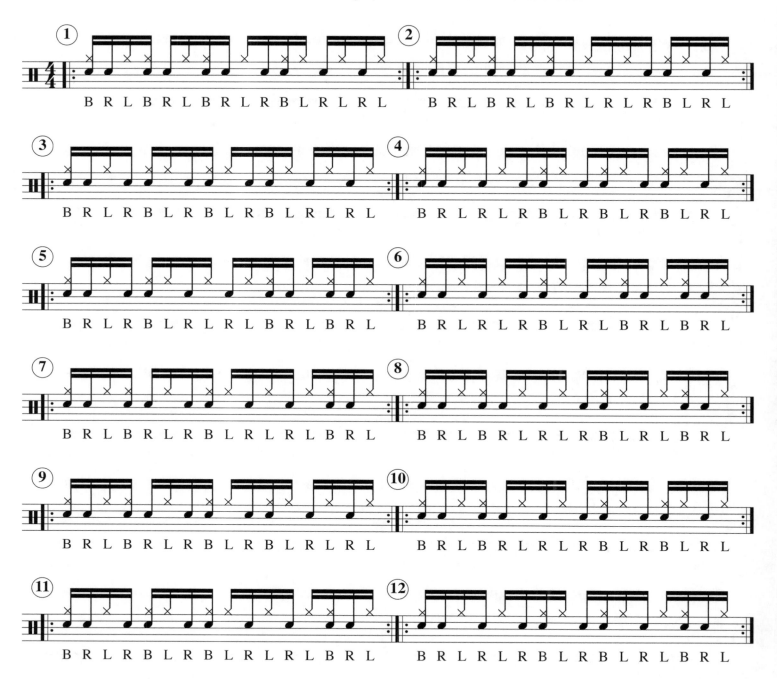

Exercise 62

Here are two examples of Latin figures derived by revoicing a rudimental sequence composed of two Swiss Army triplets, one single flammed mill, and one double flammed mill on the drumset. The first two-bar phrase uses a sequence of 4/3/3/6, producing a 2–3 cascara figure in the lead hand. The second phrase has a sequence of 3/4/6/3, producing a 3–2 cascara figure in the lead hand.

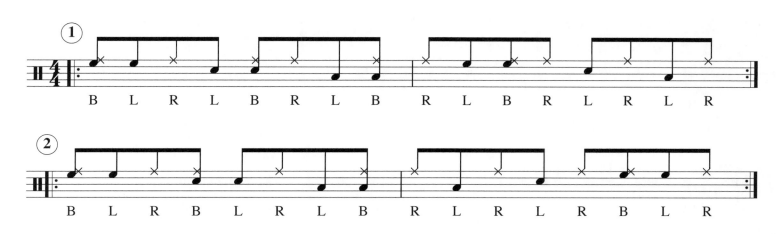

YOU CAN'T BEAT OUR DRUM BOOKS!

HAL•LEONARD DRUM PLAY-ALONG

Play your favorite songs quickly and easily with the *Drum Play-Along*™ series. Just follow the drum notation, listen to the CD to hear how the drums should sound, then play along using the separate backing tracks. The lyrics are also included for quick reference. The audio CD is playable on any CD player. For PC and Mac computer users, the CD is enhanced so you can adjust the recording to any tempo without changing the pitch!

1. Pop/Rock
Hurts So Good • Message in a Bottle • No Reply at All • Owner of a Lonely Heart • Peg • Rosanna • Separate Ways (Worlds Apart) • Swingtown.
00699742 Book/CD Pack..............................$12.95

2. Classic Rock
Barracuda • Come Together • Mississippi Queen • Radar Love • Space Truckin' • Walk This Way • White Room • Won't Get Fooled Again.
00699741 Book/CD Pack..............................$12.95

3. Hard Rock
Bark at the Moon • Detroit Rock City • Living After Midnight • Panama • Rock You like a Hurricane • Run to the Hills • Smoke on the Water • War Pigs (Interpolating Luke's Wall).
00699743 Book/CD Pack..............................$12.95

4. Modern Rock
Chop Suey! • Duality • Here to Stay • Judith • Nice to Know You • Nookie • One Step Closer • Whatever.
00699744 Book/CD Pack..............................$12.95

5. Funk
Cissy Strut • Cold Sweat, Part 1 • Fight the Power, Part 1 • Flashlight • Pick Up the Pieces • Shining Star • Soul Vaccination • Superstition.
00699745 Book/CD Pack..............................$14.99

6. '90s Rock
Alive • Been Caught Stealing • Cherub Rock • Give It Away • I'll Stick Around • Killing in the Name • Shine • Smells Like Teen Spirit.
00699746 Book/CD Pack..............................$14.99

7. Punk Rock
All the Small Things • Brain Stew (The Godzilla Remix) • Buddy Holly • Dirty Little Secret • Fat Lip • Flavor of the Weak • Lifestyles of the Rich and Famous • Self Esteem.
00699747 Book/CD Pack..............................$14.99

8. '80s Rock
Cult of Personality • Heaven's on Fire • Rock of Ages • Shake Me • Smokin' in the Boys Room • Talk Dirty to Me • We're Not Gonna Take It • You Give Love a Bad Name.
00699832 Book/CD Pack..............................$12.95

9. Big Band
Christopher Columbus • Corner Pocket • Flying Home • In the Mood • Opus One • Stompin' at the Savoy • Take the "A" Train • Woodchopper's Ball.
00699833 Book/CD Pack..............................$12.99

10. blink-182
Adam's Song • All the Small Things • Dammit • Feeling This • Man Overboard • The Rock Show • Stay Together for the Kids • What's My Age Again?
00699834 Book/CD Pack..............................$14.95

11. Jimi Hendrix Experience: Smash Hits
All Along the Watchtower • Can You See Me? • Crosstown Traffic • Fire • Foxey Lady • Hey Joe • Manic Depression • Purple Haze • Red House • Remember • Stone Free • The Wind Cries Mary.
00699835 Book/CD Pack..............................$16.95

12. The Police
Can't Stand Losing You • De Do Do Do, De Da Da Da • Don't Stand So Close to Me • Every Breath You Take • Every Little Thing She Does Is Magic • Spirits in the Material World • Synchronicity II • Walking on the Moon.
00700268 Book/CD Pack..............................$14.99

13. Steely Dan
Deacon Blues • Do It Again • FM • Hey Nineteen • Josie • My Old School • Reeling in the Years.
00700202 Book/CD Pack..............................$16.99

15. Lennon & McCartney
Back in the U.S.S.R. • Day Tripper • Drive My Car • Get Back • A Hard Day's Night • Paperback Writer • Revolution • Ticket to Ride.
00700271 Book/CD Pack..............................$14.99

17. Nirvana
About a Girl • All Apologies • Come As You Are • Dumb • Heart Shaped Box • In Bloom • Lithium • Smells like Teen Spirit.
00700273 Book/CD Pack..............................$14.95

18. Motown
Ain't Too Proud to Beg • Dancing in the Street • Get Ready • How Sweet It Is (To Be Loved by You) • I Can't Help Myself (Sugar Pie, Honey Bunch) • Sir Duke • Stop! in the Name of Love • You've Really Got a Hold on Me.
00700274 Book/CD Pack..............................$12.99

19. Rock Band: Modern Rock Edition
Are You Gonna Be My Girl • Black Hole Sun • Creep • Dani California • In Bloom • Learn to Fly • Say It Ain't So • When You Were Young.
00700707 Book/CD Pack..............................$14.95

20. Rock Band: Classic Rock Edition
Ballroom Blitz • Detroit Rock City • Don't Fear the Reaper • Gimme Shelter • Highway Star • Mississippi Queen • Suffragette City • Train Kept A-Rollin'.
00700708 Book/CD Pack..............................$14.95

21. Weezer
Beverly Hills • Buddy Holly • Dope Nose • Hash Pipe • My Name Is Jonas • Pork and Beans • Say It Ain't So • Undone – The Sweater Song.
00700959 Book/CD Pack..............................$14.99

22. Black Sabbath
Children of the Grave • Iron Man • N.I.B. • Paranoid • Sabbath, Bloody Sabbath • Sweet Leaf • War Pigs (Interpolating Luke's Wall).
00701190 Book/CD Pack..............................$16.99

23. The Who
Baba O'Riley • Bargain • Behind Blue Eyes • The Kids Are Alright • Long Live Rock • Pinball Wizard • The Seeker • Won't Get Fooled Again.
00701191 Book/CD Pack..............................$16.99

24. Pink Floyd – Dark Side of the Moon
Any Colour You Like • Brain Damage • Breathe • Eclipse • Money • Time • Us and Them.
00701612 Book/CD Pack..............................$14.99

25. Bob Marley
Could You Be Loved • Get Up Stand Up • I Shot the Sheriff • Is This Love • Jamming • No Woman No Cry • Stir It Up • Three Little Birds • Waiting in Vain.
00701703 Book/CD Pack..............................$14.99

26. Aerosmith
Back in the Saddle • Draw the Line • Dream On • Last Child • Mama Kin • Same Old Song and Dance • Sweet Emotion • Walk This Way.
00701887 Book/CD Pack..............................$14.99

27. Modern Worship
Beautiful One • Days of Elijah • Hear Our Praises • Holy Is the Lord • How Great Is Our God • I Give You My Heart • Worthy Is the Lamb • You Are Holy (Prince of Peace).
00701921 Book/CD Pack..............................$12.99

28. Avenged Sevenfold
Afterlife • Almost Easy • Bat Country • Beast and the Harlot • Nightmare • Scream • Unholy Confessions.
00702388 Book/CD Pack..............................$17.99

31. Red Hot Chili Peppers
The Adventures of Rain Dance Maggie • By the Way • Californication • Can't Stop • Dani California • Scar Tissue • Suck My Kiss • Tell Me Baby • Under the Bridge.
00702992 Book/CD Pack..............................$19.99

32. Songs for Beginners
Another One Bites the Dust • Billie Jean • Green River • Helter Skelter • I Won't Back Down • Living After Midnight • The Reason • 21 Guns.
00704204 Book/CD Pack..............................$14.99

HAL•LEONARD® CORPORATION
7777 W. BLUEMOUND RD. P.O. BOX 13819 MILWAUKEE, WI 53213

Visit Hal Leonard Online at
www.halleonard.com

0414

Prices, contents and availability subject to change without notice and may vary outside the US.